Simone Biles: A Biogr

Simone Biles is an American artistic gymnast. Biles is the 2016 Olympic individual all-around, vault and floor gold medalist. She was part of the gold medal-winning team dubbed the "Final Five" at the 2016 Summer Olympics in Rio de Janeiro. She also won the bronze medal for the balance beam during the Olympics. Biles is a three-time world all-around champion, three-time world floor champion, two-time world balance beam champion, four-time United States national all-around champion, and a member of the gold medal-winning American teams at the 2014 and 2015 World Artistic Gymnastics Championships.

Having won a combined total of nineteen Olympic and World Championship medals, Biles is the most decorated American gymnast, taking over from Shannon Miller, who had held this record since 1996. With her win in Rio, Biles became the sixth woman to have won an individual all-around title at both the World Championships and the Olympic Games. With four Olympic gold medals, Biles set an American record for most gold medals in women's gymnastics at a single Games.

Personal life

Simone Arianne Biles was born on March 14, 1997, in Columbus, Ohio, the third of four siblings. Her birth mother, Shanon Biles, was unable to care for Simone or her other children – Ashley, Tevin, and Adria – due to her drug and alcohol addiction, and the children were in and out of foster care. Simone's birth father, Kelvin Clemons, abandoned his family, struggled with addictions, and was never present in his daughter's life. Shanon's father, Ron, and his second wife, Nellie Cayetano Biles, who had two nearly-adult sons, Ron Jr. and Adam, began temporarily caring for Shanon's children in 2000, in the north Houston suburb of Spring, Texas and later in 2003 the couple officially adopted the two youngest children, Simone and Adria, and Ron's sister adopted the two eldest. Ron, Simone's father, is originally from Cleveland, and is a former air traffic controller, who served in the military with the U.S. Air Force at San Antonio's Randolph Air Force Base and later with the Federal Aviation Administration. Nellie, Simone's mother, emigrated from Belize, is a nurse and the former co-owner of a chain of fourteen Texas-based nursing homes.

Simone Biles spent all her secondary education as a homeschooler and graduated in summer 2015. She verbally committed to UCLA on August 4, 2014, announcing her decision on Twitter. She planned to defer enrollment until after the 2016 Summer Olympics in Rio de Janeiro. On July 29, 2015, she announced that she would turn professional, forfeiting her NCAA eligibility.

Biles is Catholic, and also holds Belizean citizenship through her mother. She refers to Belize as being her second home. Her sister Adria is also a gymnast.

Gymnastics career

Biles first tried gymnastics at 6 years old as part of a day-care field trip. The instructors suggested she continue with gymnastics. Biles soon enrolled in an optional training program at Bannon's Gymnastix. She began training with coach Aimee Boorman at age 8.

Biles began her career on July 1, 2011, at the 2011 American Classic in Houston. She placed third all-around, first on vault and balance beam, fourth on floor exercise, and eighth on uneven bars. Later that month, Biles competed at the 2011 U.S. Classic in Chicago, Illinois, where she placed twentieth all-around, fifth on balance beam and floor exercise.

In 2012, Biles switched from public school to home schooling. The change allowed her to increase her training from approximately 20 hours a week to 32. Biles credited the increased training time with her improved success during the 2012 season.

Biles' first meet of 2012 was again the American Classic in Huntsville, Texas, where she placed first all-around and on vault, tied for second on floor exercise, placed third on balance beam and fourth on uneven bars. Biles' placement in the American Classic secured her spot to compete at the 2012 USA Gymnastics National Championships. She later competed at the 2012 U.S. Classic in Chicago. She finished first all-around and on vault, second on floor exercise, and sixth on balance beam. In June, she made her second appearance at the USA Gymnastics National Championships, this time in St. Louis, Missouri. She finished third all-around, first on vault, and sixth on uneven bars, balance beam, and floor exercise. After this performance, Biles was named to the United States Junior National Team.

Biles' senior international debut was in March at the 2013 American Cup, an FIG World Cup event. She and Katelyn Ohashi were named as replacements for Elizabeth Price and 2012 Olympic gold medalist Kyla Ross, both of whom withdrew from the competition because of injuries. Biles led for two rotations but finished second behind her teammate, Ohashi, after a fall off the beam.

Biles immediately went on to compete at the 2013 City of Jesolo Trophy in Jesolo, Italy, where she took the all-around, vault, balance beam, and floor exercise titles in addition to contributing to the United States' team gold medal. She and the U.S. delegation then competed at an international tri-meet in Chemnitz, Germany, against teams from Germany and Romania. The U.S. again won the team gold. In addition, Biles won the vault, balance beam, and floor titles, but tied for second in the all-around behind Ross after a fall on the uneven bars.

In July, Biles competed at the 2013 U.S. Classic. She performed poorly, falling several times, and did not compete vault after tweaking her ankle on the floor exercise. Afterward, she was invited to a private camp with the national team coordinator, Marta Karolyi, and consulted a sports psychologist. Biles went on to compete at the 2013 USA Gymnastics National Championships in August, where she was crowned the national all-around champion ahead of Ross. Biles also won silver on all four individual events. After the USA Gymnastics National Championships, she was named to the Senior National Team and was invited to the qualifying camp for the 2013 World Artistic Gymnastics Championships in Texas, where she was named to the World Championships team.

In October, Biles competed at the 2013 World Artistic Gymnastics Championships in Antwerp, Belgium. She qualified first in the all-around, second to the vault final, sixth to the uneven bars final, fifth to the balance beam final, and first to the floor final, making her the first American gymnast to qualify to the all-around and all four event finals since Shannon Miller in 1991. Biles competed cleanly during the women's individual all-around and won the competition with a score of 60.216, almost a point ahead of silver medalist Ross and almost a point and a half better than the bronze medalist, 2010 world all-around champion Aliya Mustafina. Biles became the seventh American woman and the first African-American to win the world all-around title. In event finals, she won silver on the vault, behind defending world champion and Olympic silver medalist McKayla Maroney and ahead of 2008 Olympic gold medalist Hong Un Jong of North Korea; bronze on balance beam, behind Mustafina and Ross; and gold on the floor exercise, ahead of Italy's Vanessa Ferrari and Romania's Larisa Iordache. She finished fourth in the uneven bars final, behind China's Huang Huidan, Ross, and Mustafina.

Biles missed the start of season due to an aggravated shoulder injury, sitting out the 2014 AT&T American Cup and the 2014 Pacific Rim Championships. Biles 2014 debut came at the U.S. Classic in Chicago. She won the all-around by a wide margin and also took first place on vault, beam , and floor. At the 2014 USA Gymnastics National Championships, Biles repeated as national all-around champion after two days of competition, finishing more than four points ahead of silver medalist Ross, despite a fall from the balance beam during her final routine of the meet. She won the gold on vault and floor, tied for the silver on balance beam with Alyssa Baumann, and finished fourth on the uneven bars. She was once again named to the Senior National Team.

On September 17, Biles was selected to compete at the 2014 World Artistic Gymnastics Championships in Nanning, China. She dominated the preliminary round despite a major error on the uneven bars, qualifying in first place to the all-around, vault, beam, and floor finals, in addition to contributing to the U.S. team's first-place qualification into the team final. During the team final, Biles led the United States to its second consecutive world team championship, which they won over the second-place Chinese team by nearly seven points. In the all-around, Biles performed cleanly on all four events, bettering her bars score from qualifications by over a point, and won her second consecutive world all-around title ahead of two good friends, Ross and Iordache. Biles became the second American woman to repeat as world all-around champion, following Miller , and the first woman of any nationality to do so since Russia's Svetlana Khorkina . She also received extra press when a video of her fleeing from a bee on the podium during the all-around award ceremony went viral. Biles finished behind North Korea's Hong Un Jong in the vault competition, taking her second consecutive silver medal in that event, but went on to win the gold in the balance beam final ahead of China's Bai Yawen and the gold in the floor exercise final, again, ahead of Iordache. This brought her total of World Championship gold medals to six, the most ever by an American gymnast, surpassing Miller's five. After the world championships, she was named one of ESPNW's Impact 25 and chosen as Sportswoman of the Year by the Women's Sports Foundation.

Biles competed at the 2015 AT&T American Cup at AT&T Stadium in Arlington, Texas on March 7. She placed first with a score of 62.299, 4.467 points ahead of second-place finisher U.S. teammate Mykayla Skinner. Later that month, Biles was nominated for the James E. Sullivan Award. She ended the month at the 2015 City of Jesolo Trophy, winning the all-around title with 62.100.

On July 25, she competed at the U.S. Classic and finished first in the all-around, ahead of 2012 Olympic all-around champion Gabby Douglas and Maggie Nichols, with a score of 62.400. On the beam, she scored a 15.250 and took first at the event, ahead of Douglas and 2012 Olympic beam bronze medalist Aly Raisman. She scored a 16.050 on the floor and claimed first on the event, 1.050 points ahead of Douglas and also ahead of Nichols and Bailie Key. She had a small hop on her Amanar vault and scored a 16.000. She then scored 15.150

on her second vault, to score an average of 15.575 and place first in the event, ahead of 2014 Worlds vault bronze medalist and teammate MyKayla Skinner, who averaged 14.950. Biles ended on bars and scored a 15.100 to claim the all-around title. She placed fourth in the event behind 2014 Worlds teammate Madison Kocian, Douglas, and Key.

On July 29, shortly after her performance at the U.S. Classic, Biles announced that she would be turning pro, thus forfeiting her chance to compete for the UCLA Bruins gymnastics team. She signed with Octagon, who also supports fellow American gymnast Aly Raisman and Olympic swimmer Michael Phelps. At the 2015 U.S. National Championships, Biles secured her third all-around national title, becoming only the second woman to ever do so, 23 years after Kim Zmeskal .

Biles, along with Douglas, Dowell, Kocian, Nichols, Raisman, and Skinner, was selected to represent the United States at the 2015 World Artistic Gymnastics Championships in Glasgow, Scotland. Biles once again qualified in first place to the all-around, vault, beam, and floor finals. Her uneven bars score would have qualified her in

8th place to that final as well, but she was excluded, as per the rules, after teammates Kocian and Douglas qualified ahead of her. In team finals, she helped the United States team win their third consecutive gold medal at a World Championships event. During the all-around final, Biles performed below her usual standard, taking a large hop on vault, landing out of bounds on floor , and grasping the beam to prevent a fall. However, her final score of 60.399 was more than enough to secure the title with her largest margin of victory yet . With that victory, Biles became the first woman to win three consecutive all-around titles in World Gymnastics Championships history. During day one of event finals, Biles competed on vault, taking bronze behind Maria Paseka and Hong Un Jon . On day two, she competed on balance beam and floor exercise, retaining her world title on both events by large margins. This brought Biles' total World Championships medal count to 14, the most for any American, and total gold medal count to 10, the most for any woman in World Championships history.

As of November 11, 2015, she was a Nike-sponsored athlete – announcing this news through Twitter.

Biles was named Team USA Female Olympic Athlete of the Year in December 2015, making her the fourth gymnast to win the honor.

Biles went into the 2016 season as a fourth-year senior and the reigning National champion. On December 17, 2015, USA Gymnastics announced that she would compete at the 2016 Pacific Rim Gymnastics Championships, in April 2016 in Everett, Washington.

At her first competition of the year, the Pacific Rim Championships, Biles came home with the all-around title and had the highest score on vault , floor exercise , and balance beam. Additionally, the US came home with the team title by a wide margin. Biles did not compete in the event finals.

On June 4, Biles competed at the Secret US Classic, on the uneven bars and beam. She did not compete vault or floor exercise. She achieved the highest score on beam, a 15.650, and also received a 15.1 on bars, good enough for 5th in the event.

In the following weeks, Biles competed at the 2016 USA Gymnastics National Championships. Her vault and floor routines all received marks of at least sixteen all four times, and she received the national titles of both, respectively. On bars, she scored 14.750 and an average of 14.925, just shy of a 15 average, and a bronze for the event. On beam she again did very well, with very minor struggles on Day 2, again winning another medal. She won the all-around title by a wide margin of 3.9 points over Aly Raisman. Her two-day total was 125 points even, with an all-around average of 62.5 points.

On July 10, Biles was named to the team for the 2016 Olympics, alongside Gabby Douglas, Laurie Hernandez, Madison Kocian and Aly Raisman.

In September 2016, Biles' medical information was released following the Russian cyber espionage group Fancy Bear's hack into the World Anti Doping Agency. Biles then disclosed on Twitter that she has attention deficit hyperactivity disorder and was permitted to take medication for it, having applied for and received a Therapeutic Use Exemption.

In 2016 she was chosen as one of BBC's 100 Women, and as the 2016 espnW IMPACT25 Woman of the Year. She was also one of the finalists for Time magazine's 2016 Person of the Year. Biles was also nominated for a 2016 ESPY award for Best Female Athlete along with

Elena Delle Donne, Katie Ledecky, and Breanna Stewart; Stewart won the award.

Biles appeared with gymnasts Dominique Dawes and Nadia Comăneci in a commercial for Tide called "The Evolution of Power" prior to the 2016 Summer Olympics.

On August 7, Biles competed in the Women's Qualification at the 2016 Summer Olympics. She scored a 16.050 on the vault, a 15.000 on the uneven bars, a 15.633 on the balance beam, and a 15.733 on the floor exercise. Along with the team final, she individually qualified into the all-around, vault, balance beam, and floor exercise finals. On August 9, Biles won her first Olympic gold medal in the gymnastics team event. She also won the gold medal individual all-around on August 11, with teammate Aly Raisman winning the silver and Russia's Aliya Mustafina claiming the bronze. Biles had a total score of 62.198 with 15.866 on the vault, 14.966 on the uneven bars, 15.433 on the balance beam, and 15.933 on the floor. Biles had the highest scores on vault, balance beam, and floor; she had the only score over 15 on balance beam in the finals. In the women's vault, she won her second individual gold medal with a score of 15.966, more than 0.7

points ahead of second-place finisher Maria Paseka of Russia and third-place finisher Giulia Steingruber of Switzerland. In the women's balance beam final, she grabbed the beam, scoring a 14.733. Despite her mistake, wobbly routines from France's Marine Boyer, Brazil's Flavia Saraiva, China's Fan Yilin, Romania's Catalina Ponor, and Canadian Isabela Onyshko allowed her to grab bronze behind teammate Laurie Hernandez who won silver and Sanne Wevers of the Netherlands. In the women's floor exercise final, she won gold with a score of 15.966. Teammate Aly Raisman won silver with a score of 15.500 and Amy Tinkler of Great Britain won bronze. She contributed to an historic feat for the gymnastics team, with USA claiming a medal on every event for the first time since 1984.

With four Olympic gold medals, Biles set a new American record for most gold medals in women's gymnastics at a single Games, and equalled a number of other records with her medals won in Rio. Biles' win of four gold medals was the first instance of a quadruple gold medallist in women's gymnastics at a single Games since Ecaterina Szabo in 1984, and the fifth overall, after Larisa Latynina , Agnes Keleti , Věra Čáslavská and Szabo. Biles became the sixth female gymnast to have won an individual all-around title at both the World

Championships and the Olympic Games; the others being Larisa Latynina, Věra Čáslavská, Ludmilla Tourischeva, Elena Shushunova and Lilia Podkopayeva. Biles is the first female gymnast since Lilia Podkopayeva in 1996 to win the all around gold as well as an event final gold, and the first female gymnast since Podkopayeva to win the Olympic all around title while holding the World and European/American individual all around titles. Biles joins Latynina , Čáslavská and Tourischeva , as the fourth female gymnast to win every major all-around title in an Olympic cycle.

Biles now joins Mary Lou Retton in 1984, Shannon Miller in 1992 and Nastia Liukin in 2008 in winning five medals at a single Olympic Games, along with Szabo , Nadia Comaneci and Karin Janz . Olga Mostepanova also won five gold medals at the Alternate Olympics in 1984. The overall record for most women's Olympic gymnastics medals at a single games , remains six medals .

Biles and her teammate Gabby Douglas are the only African American female U.S. gymnasts to win both the individual all-around gold and team gold at the same Olympic games. Douglas won both in the 2012 London games.

She was chosen by Team USA to be the flag bearer for the closing ceremonies. She was the first American female gymnast to be given the honor.

Competitive history

The 2016 Summer Olympics , officially known as the Games of the XXXI Olympiad and commonly known as Rio 2016, was a major international multi-sport event held in Rio de Janeiro, Brazil, from 5 August to 21 August 2016.

More than 11,000 athletes from 205 National Olympic Committees, including first time entrants Kosovo, South Sudan, and the Refugee Olympic Team, took part. With 306 sets of medals, the games featured 28 Olympic sports, including rugby sevens and golf, which were added to the Olympic program in 2009. These sporting events took place at 33 venues in the host city, and at five in São Paulo, Belo Horizonte, Salvador, Brasília, and Manaus.

These were the first Summer Olympic Games under the International Olympic Committee presidency of Thomas Bach. The host city Rio de Janeiro was announced at the 121st IOC Session in Copenhagen, Denmark, on 2 October 2009. Rio became the first South American city to host the Summer Olympics. These were the first games to be held in a Portuguese-speaking country, the first to be held entirely in the host country's winter, the first since 1968 to be held in Latin America, and the first since 2000 to be held in the Southern Hemisphere.

The lead-up to these Games was marked by controversies, including the instability of the country's federal government; health and safety concerns surrounding the Zika virus and significant pollution in the Guanabara Bay; and a doping scandal involving Russia, which has affected the participation of its athletes in the Games.

The United States topped the medal table for the fifth time in the past six Summer Olympics, winning the most golds and most medals overall , as well as its 1,000th Olympic gold medal overall. Great Britain finished second and became the first country in the history of the modern Olympics to increase its tally of medals in the subsequent games after being the host nation. China finished third. Host country Brazil won seven gold medals, its most at any single Summer Olympics, finishing in thirteenth place. Fiji, Jordan, Kosovo, Puerto

Rico, Singapore, Tajikistan, Ivory Coast and Vietnam each won their first gold medals, as did the group of Independent Olympic Athletes .

Bidding process

The bidding process for the 2016 Olympic Games was officially launched on 16 May 2007. The first step for each city was to submit an initial application to the International Olympic Committee by 13 September 2007, confirming their intention to bid. Completed official bid files, containing answers to a 25-question IOC form, were to be submitted by each applicant city by 14 January 2008. Four candidate cities were chosen for the shortlist on 4 June 2008: Chicago, Madrid, Rio de Janeiro and Tokyo, which hosted the 1964 Summer Olympics and will host again in 2020. The IOC did not promote Doha to the candidature phase, despite scoring higher than selected candidate city Rio de Janeiro, because of their intent of hosting the Olympics in October, outside of the IOC's sporting calendar. Prague and Baku also failed to make the cut.

Nawal El Moutawakel of Morocco headed the 10-member Evaluation Commission, having also chaired the evaluation commission for the 2012 Summer Olympics bids. The commission made on-site inspections in the second quarter of 2009. They issued a comprehensive technical appraisal for IOC members on 2 September, one month before elections.

Many restrictions are in place designed to prevent bidding cities from communicating with or influencing directly the 115 voting members. Cities may not invite any IOC member to visit nor may they send anything that could be construed as a gift. Nonetheless, bidding cities invest large sums in their PR and media programs in an attempt to indirectly influence the IOC members by garnering domestic support, support from sports media and general international media.

The final voting was held on 2 October 2009, in Copenhagen with Madrid and Rio de Janeiro perceived as favourites to land the games. Chicago and Tokyo were eliminated after the first and second rounds of voting, respectively, while Rio de Janeiro took a significant lead over Madrid heading into the final round. The lead held and Rio de Janeiro was announced as host of 2016 Summer Olympics.

Development and preparation

On 26 June 2011, it was reported on AroundTheRings.com that Roderlei Generali, the COO of the Rio de Janeiro Organizing

Committee for the Olympic Games, resigned just one year after taking the job at ROOC. This comes just five months after CCO Flávio Pestana quit for personal reasons. Pestana withdrew later during the 2012 Summer Paralympics. Renato Ciuchin was then appointed as COO.

Events took place at eighteen existing venues, nine new venues constructed specifically for the Games, and seven temporary venues.

Each event was held in one of four geographically segregated Olympic clusters: Barra, Copacabana, Deodoro, and Maracanã. The same was done for the 2007 Pan American Games. Several of the venues were located at the Barra Cluster Olympic Park. Athletes could access their venues in shorter than 10 minutes and about 75 percent could do so in less than 25 minutes. Of the 34 competition locales, eight have undergone permanent works, seven are limited, and nine are perpetual legacy venues.

The largest venue at the games in terms of seating capacity was the 74,738-seat Maracanã Stadium, which served as the ceremonies venue and site of the football finals. The second largest stadium was the 60,000-seat Estádio Olímpico João Havelange, which hosted track and field events.

The athletes' village was said to be the largest in Olympic history. Fittings included about 80,000 chairs, 70,000 tables, 29,000 mattresses, 60,000 clothes hangers, 6,000 television sets and 10,000 smartphones.

The Barra Olympic Park is a cluster of nine sporting venues in Barra da Tijuca, in the west zone of Rio de Janeiro, Brazil. The site of the Olympic Park was formerly occupied by the Autódromo Internacional Nelson Piquet, also known as Jacarepaguá.

The nine venues within the Olympic Park are: Carioca Arena 1: basketball ; Carioca Arena 2: wrestling, judo ; Carioca Arena 3: fencing, taekwondo ; Future Arena: handball ; Maria Lenk Aquatics Centre: diving, synchronised swimming, water polo ; Olympic Aquatics Stadium: swimming, water polo play-offs ; Olympic Tennis Centre: tennis ; Rio Olympic Arena: gymnastics ; and Rio Olympic Velodrome: track cycling .

As well as the Estádio Olímpico João Havelange and Maracanã and in Rio de Janeiro, football matches took place at 5 venues in the cities of São Paulo, Belo Horizonte, Salvador, Brasília and Manaus.

Rio's historical downtown is undergoing a large-scale urban waterfront revitalization project called Porto Maravilha. It covers 5 km2 in area. The project aims to redevelop the port area, increasing the city center's attractiveness and enhancing Rio's competitive position in the global economy. The urban renovation involves: 700 km of public networks for water supply, sanitation, drainage, electricity, gas and telecom; 4 km of tunnels; 70 km of roads; 650 km2 of sidewalks; 17 km of bike path; 15,000 trees; three sanitation treatment plants. As part of this renovation, a new tram was built from the Santos Dumont Airport to Rodoviária Novo Rio. It was due to open in April 2016.

The Games required more than 200 kilometres of security fencing. A 15,000 square metre warehouse in Barra da Tijuca in western Rio was used to assemble and supply the furniture and fittings for the Olympic Village. A second warehouse of 90,000 square metres, located in Duque de Caxias near the roads that provide access to the venues, contained all the equipment needed for the sporting events.

The medal design was unveiled on 15 June 2016; they were produced by the Casa da Moeda do Brasil. The bronze and silver medals contained 30% recycled materials, while the gold medals were produced using gold that had been mined and extracted using means that met a series of sustainability criteria, such as being extracted without the use of mercury. The medals feature a wreath design, while the obverse, as is traditional, features Nike, the Greek goddess of victory. They were accompanied by a wooden carrying box, while medallists also received a trophy of the Games' emblem.

As an aspect of its bid, Rio's organizing committee committed to a focus on sustainability and environmental protection as a theme of these Games, going on to dub them a "Green Games for a Blue Planet". Organizers intended to, as legacy projects, introduce a wider array of public transport options, upgrade the infrastructure of the favelas to provide improved transport and access to utilities, upgrade Rio's sewer system in order to remediate the level of pollution in the Guanabara Bay. and plant 24 million seedlings to offset the expected carbon emissions of the Games. However, some of these projects were met with delays or faced with economic shortfalls, which led some critics to believe that Rio would not be able to accomplish them.

The focus on environmental protection also influenced the implementation of certain Olympic protocols: the Olympic cauldron was designed to be smaller than previous iterations in order to reduce emissions, and utilizes a kinetic sculpture to enhance its appearance in lieu of a larger body of flames. The bronze and silver medals, as well as ribbons on all medals, incorporate recycled materials, and athletes were not presented with flowers during medal ceremonies, as had been traditionally done at prior Olympics . Organizers considered the practice to be wasteful since they were often thrown away, and "would struggle to survive in the tropical Brazilian climate" if kept. The podiums were also designed so that their materials could be recycled to make furniture. The Future Arena, host of handball competitions, was designed as a modular temporary venue whose components can be reconstructed to build schools.

Portions of the opening ceremony were also dedicated to the issue of climate change.

The Olympic flame was lit at the temple of Hera in Olympia on 21 April 2016, the traditional start of the Greek phase of the torch relay. On 27 April the flame was handed over to the Brazilian organizers at a ceremony at the Panathenaic Stadium in Athens. A brief stop was made in Switzerland to visit the IOC headquarters and the Olympic Museum in Lausanne as well as the United Nations Office at Geneva.

The torch relay began its Brazilian journey on 3 May at the capital Brasília. The torch relay visited more than 300 Brazilian cities , with the last part held in the city of Rio de Janeiro, lighting the cauldron during the 2016 Summer Olympics opening ceremony on 5 August.

The ticket prices were announced on 16 September 2014, all of which were sold in Brazilian reais . A total of 7.5 million tickets were to be sold in total, with ticket prices ranging from BRL 40 for many events to BRL 4,600 for the most expensive seats at the opening ceremony. About 3.8 million of these tickets were available for BRL 70 or less.

The Games

The opening ceremony took place in the Maracanã Stadium on 5 August 2016, and was directed by Fernando Meirelles, Daniela Thomas and Andrucha Waddington. The ceremony highlighted aspects of Brazilian history and culture, and featured a segment narrated by Fernanda Montenegro and Judi Dench with an appeal to environmental conservation and preventing global warming. The ceremony also featured the inaugural presentation of the Olympic Laurel, an honour bestowed by the IOC to those that have made "significant achievements in education, culture, development and peace through sport", to Kipchoge "Kip" Keino. The Games were officially opened by Acting President of Brazil Michel Temer.

The Olympic cauldron was lit by Vanderlei Cordeiro de Lima, the men's marathon bronze medallist at the 2004 Summer Olympics who was also awarded the Pierre de Coubertin medal for sportsmanship by the IOC after being attacked by a spectator and losing his lead. The cauldron was originally expected to be lit by Brazilian footballer Pelé, but he declined to participate due to health problems. A public cauldron was lit in front of the Candelária Church by a 14-year-old participant in Rio's Vila Olimpica program—which provides access to training facilities to disadvantaged youth.

The 2016 Summer Olympic programme featured 28 sports encompassing 306 events. The number of events in each discipline is noted in parentheses.

In April 2008, the IOC began accepting applications for two new sports to be introduced to the Olympic programme, which included baseball and softball , karate, squash, golf, roller sports, and rugby union all applied to be included. Formal presentations were held for the IOC executive board in June 2009. In August, the executive board initially gave its approval to rugby sevens—a seven-player version of rugby union—by a majority vote, thus removing baseball, roller sports, and squash from contention. Among the remaining three—golf, karate, and softball—the board approved golf as a result of consultation. The final decision regarding the remaining two sports was made on 9 October 2009, the final day of the 121st IOC Session. A new system was in place at this session; a sport now needed only a simple majority from the full IOC committee for approval rather than the two-thirds majority previously required.

The International Sailing Federation announced in May 2012 that windsurfing would be replaced at the 2016 Olympics by kitesurfing, but this decision was reversed in November. The IOC announced in January 2013 that it would review the status of cycling events, following Lance Armstrong's admission of using performance-enhancing drugs and accusations that cycling's governing body had covered up doping.

All 206 National Olympic Committees have qualified at least one athlete. The first three nations to qualify athletes for the Games were Germany, Great Britain, and the Netherlands who each qualified four athletes for the team dressage by winning medals in the team event at the 2014 FEI World Equestrian Games.

As host nation, Brazil has received automatic entry for some sports including in all cycling disciplines and six places for weightlifting events. The 2016 Summer Olympics are the first games in which Kosovo and South Sudan are eligible to participate. Bulgarian and Russian weightlifters were banned from Rio Olympics for numerous anti-doping violations.

Kuwait was banned in October 2015 for the second time in five years over government interference in the country's Olympic committee.

Due to the European migrant crisis and other reasons, the International Olympic Committee allowed athletes to compete as Independent Olympians under the Olympic Flag. In the previous Olympic Games, refugees were ineligible to compete because of their inability to represent their home NOCs. On 2 March 2016, the IOC finalized plans for a specific Refugee Olympic Team ; out of 43 refugee athletes deemed potentially eligible, 10 were chosen to form the team.

Due to the suspension of the National Olympic Committee of Kuwait, participants from Kuwait were allowed to participate under the Olympic Flag as Independent Olympic Athletes.

In November 2015, Russia was provisionally suspended from all international athletic competitions by the International Association of Athletics Federations following a World Anti-Doping Agency report into a doping program in the country. The IAAF announced that it would allow individual Russian athletes to apply for "exceptional eligibility" to participate in the Games as "neutral" athletes, if it were independently verified that they had not engaged in doping nor in the Russian doping program.

On 24 July 2016, the IOC rejected the IAAF and WADA's recommendations to allow clean athletes to compete neutrally, stating that the Olympic Charter "does not foresee such 'neutral athletes'" and that it was up to each country's National Olympic Committee to decide which athletes would be competing.

During the Games some countries and continents had a national house. These temporary meeting places for supporters, athletes and other followers were located throughout Rio de Janeiro.

Source

This is currently based on the schedule released on the same day as ticket sales began, 31 March 2015.

Twenty-seven world records and ninety-one Olympic records were set during the 2016 Summer Olympics. The records were set in archery, athletics, canoeing, cycling track, modern pentathlon, rowing, shooting, swimming and weightlifting.

The top ten listed NOCs by number of gold medals are listed below. Host nation Brazil finished in 13th place with a total of 19 medals .

To sort this table by nation, total medal count, or any other column, click on the icon next to the column title.

A number of events, most notably in aquatics, beach volleyball, and track and field, were scheduled with sessions and matches occurring as late as 22:00 to 00:00 BRT. These scheduling practices were influenced primarily by United States broadcast rightsholder NBC , as well as the main Brazilian rightsholder Rede Globo. As Brasília time is only one hour ahead of the U.S. Eastern Time Zone, certain marquee events were scheduled so they could occur during the lucrative U.S. primetime hours , allowing them to be broadcast live on the U.S. east coast as opposed to being delayed. This practice was also to the benefit of domestic broadcaster Rede Globo, which elected to not preempt its widely viewed lineup of primetime telenovelas for the Games. However, Globo did preempt its telenovelas for the opening ceremony; a Brazilian television critic noted that Globo very rarely preempts its telenovelas.

The closing ceremony of the 2016 Summer Olympics was held on 21 August 2016 from 20:00 to 22:50 BRT at the Maracanã Stadium. As per traditional Olympic protocol, the ceremony featured cultural presentations from both the current and following host countries, as well as closing remarks by International Olympic Committee president Thomas Bach and the leader of the Games' organizing committee Carlos Arthur Nuzman, the official handover of the Olympic flag from Rio de Janeiro mayor Eduardo Paes to Tokyo governor Yuriko Koike, whose city will host the 2020 Summer Olympics, and the extinguishing of the Olympic flame.

The creative director for the ceremony was Rosa Magalhães. Amid heavy rainfall, the ceremony began with interpretive dancers representing various landmarks in the host city. Martinho da Vila then performed a rendition of the classic song "Carinhoso " by Pixinguinha. In another segment, introducing the athletes, pop singer Roberta Sá channeled Carmen Miranda, the fruit-headdress-wearing, midcentury Hollywood diva who endures as a beloved camp figure. The Parade of Flags followed shortly after a choir of 27 children, representing the states of Brazil, sang the Brazilian national anthem.

The Oxford Olympics Study 2016 estimates the outturn cost of the Rio 2016 Summer Olympics at USD 4.6 billion in 2015-dollars. This includes sports-related costs, that is, operational costs incurred by the organizing committee for the purpose of staging the Games, of which the largest components are technology, transportation, workforce, and administration costs, while other operational costs include security, catering, ceremonies, and medical services, and direct capital costs incurred by the host city and country or private investors to build the competition venues, the Olympic village, international broadcast center, and media and press center, which are required to host the Games. Indirect capital costs are not included, such as for road, rail, or airport infrastructure, or for hotel upgrades or other business investment incurred in preparation for the Games but not directly related to staging the Games. The Rio Olympics' cost of USD 4.6 billion compares with costs of USD 15 billion for London 2012 and USD 6.8 billion for Beijing 2008. Average cost for the Summer Games since 1960 is USD 5.2 billion.

Broadcasting

Olympic Broadcasting Services served as the host broadcaster for these Games; produced from a total of 52 mobile units, OBS distributed 40,000 hours of television footage and 60,000 hours of digital footage of the Games to its international rightsholders; for the first time in Olympic history, digital-oriented footage exceeded the amount of television-oriented footage. The International Broadcast Centre was constructed in the Barra da Tijuca cluster. NHK and OBS once again filmed portions of the Games, including the opening ceremony and selected events, in 8K resolution video. Additionally, expanding upon a 180-degree trial at the 2016 Winter Youth Olympics, 85 hours of video content were originated in 360-degree virtual reality formats. In the United States, NBC offered 4K content, downconverted from the 8K footage and with HDR and Dolby Atmos support, to participating television providers. Owing to their expertise in domestic broadcasts of the new sports introduced in Rio, NBC and Sky New Zealand staff handled the production of the golf and rugby sevens events on behalf of OBS.

In August 2009, the IOC reached a deal to sell domestic broadcast rights to the 2016 Summer Olympics to Grupo Globo. Replacing Rede Record, the deal covers free-to-air coverage on Rede Globo, pay TV, and digital rights to the Games. In turn, Globo sub-licensed partial free-to-air rights to Rede Record, along with Rede Bandeirantes. IOC board member Richard Carrión described the agreement as "unprecedented", touting that "by working with Brazil's leading media organizations, we are confident that this represents a great deal for Olympic fans in the region. There will be a huge increase in the amount of Olympic action broadcast, both during and outside Games time, and Brazilians will have more choice of how, when and where they follow their Olympic Games."

Marketing

The official mascots of the 2016 Summer Olympics and Paralympics were unveiled on 24 November 2014. They were created by Sao Paulo-based animation company Birdo. The Olympic mascot Vinicius, named after musician Vinicius de Moraes, represents Brazilian wildlife and carries design traits of cats, monkeys, and birds. According to their fictional backgrounds, the mascots "were both born from the joy of Brazilians after it was announced that Rio would host the Games." Brand director Beth Lula stated that the mascots are intended to reflect the diversity of Brazil's culture and people. The names of the mascots were determined by a public vote whose results were announced on 14 December 2014; the names, which reference the co-writers of the song "The Girl from Ipanema", won over two other sets of names, tallying 44 percent of 323,327 votes. At the Olympic wrestling events, coaches were given plush dolls of Vinicius to throw into the ring when they wished to challenge a referee's call.

The official emblem for the 2016 Summer Olympics was designed by the Brazilian agency Tatíl Design and unveiled on 31 December 2010, winning in a competition against 139 agencies. The logo represents three figures joined at their arms and feet, with the overall shape reflecting that of Sugarloaf Mountain. The emblem was also designed to have a three-dimensional form, which designer Fred Gelli claimed made it the "first 3D logo in the history of the Olympics."

The logo has been noted as evoking Henri Matisse's painting Dance. There were also allegations by the Colorado-based Telluride Foundation that the logo had been plagiarized from its own. While also consisting of several figures linked in motion, the Telluride Foundation logo contains four figures. This is not the first time that the foundation had alleged plagiarism of its logo by a Brazilian event; in 2004, the linked figures element had been copied for the logo of Carnival celebrations in Salvador. Gelli defended the allegations, stating that the concept of figures linked in embrace was not inherently original as it was "an ancient reference" and "in the collective unconscious". Gelli cited Dance as an influence of the logo's concept, and stated that the designers had intentionally aimed to make the interpretation of the concept as dissimilar to others as possible.

Concerns and controversies

An ongoing outbreak of the mosquito-borne Zika virus in Brazil raised fears regarding its potential impact on athletes and visitors. To prevent puddles of stagnant water that allow mosquitoes to breed, organizers announced plans to perform daily inspections of Olympic venues. Zika virus transmission was also attributed to inefficient sewage treatment in the area—an issue that was also in the process of being addressed for the Games. In May 2016, a group of 150 physicians and scientists sent an open letter to the World Health Organization, calling upon them to, according to co-author Arthur Caplan, have "an open, transparent discussion of the risks of holding the Olympics as planned in Brazil". The WHO dismissed the request, stating that "cancelling or changing the location of the 2016 Olympics will not significantly alter the international spread of Zika virus", and that there was "no public health justification" for postponing them. Some athletes did not attend the Games because of the epidemic. On 2 September 2016, the World Health Organization reported that there were no confirmed cases of Zika among athletes or visitors during the Olympics.

The Guanabara Bay, whose waters were used for sailing and windsurfing competitions, is heavily polluted. Among the chief causes of the pollution are uncollected trash fed into the bay via polluted rivers and slums along the coast. Pollution of the Guanabara has been a long-term issue. Officials promised at the Earth Summit in 1992 that they would begin to address the pollution but previous attempts to do so have been insufficient. As an aspect of their bid for the Games, Rio once again committed to making efforts towards cleaning the bay. However, some of these proposed initiatives have faced budgetary issues. Prior to these efforts, only 17% of Rio's sewage was treated; this raw sewage also leaked into the bay. Although Mayor of Rio Eduardo Paes stated that the city may not be able to reach its goal of having 80% of sewage treated, at least 60% of sewage was treated by March 2016, with a projected goal of 65% of sewage being treated by the time the Olympics started.

In 2014, Operation Car Wash, an investigation by the Federal Police of Brazil, uncovered unprecedented money laundering and corruption at the state-controlled oil company Petrobras. In early 2015, a series of protests against alleged corruption by the government of President Dilma Rousseff began in Brazil, triggered by revelations that numerous politicians were involved in the Petrobras affair. By early 2016, the scandal had escalated into a full-blown political crisis affecting not only President Rousseff, but also former President Luiz Inácio Lula da Silva, resulting in massive demonstrations all over the country involving millions of protesters, both anti and pro-Rousseff. At the same time, Brazil faced its worst economic recession since the 1990s, raising questions about whether the country was adequately prepared for the Games against a volatile political and economic backdrop. On 12 May, President Rousseff was stripped of her powers and duties for 180 days, after an impeachment vote in the Federal Senate, thus Vice President Michel Temer acted as acting president during the Games.

Rio's crime problems also received renewed attention after it was awarded the Games; Mayor Paes stated that the city was facing "big issues" in heightening security, but that such concerns and issues were presented to the IOC throughout the bidding process. The governor of the state of Rio de Janeiro also highlighted the fact that London faced security problems, with a terrorist attack occurring just one day after it was awarded the 2012 Summer Olympics. The estimate was that 5,000 men of the National Public Security Force and 22,000 military officers, in addition to the fixed quota of Rio January, would act during the Olympic Games. On 21 July 2016, two weeks before the scheduled start of the Games, the Brazilian Federal Police broke up an Islamic jihadist terrorist ring, with 10 ISIL associates arrested and two more on the run.

While the whole city underwent major infrastructure improvements, there were concerns that some of the projects would never materialise. On 21 April—the day that the Olympic torch was lit—a 50 metres section of the Tim Maia bike path, crossing the Oscar Niemeyer Avenue in São Conrado neighborhood and a part of the legacy of the games, was hit by a giant wave and collapsed, causing the death of two pedestrians and injuries to three more. The athlete's village has been described as the largest in Olympic history, but two weeks before the Olympics opened, officials also described it as "unliveable" and unsafe because of major plumbing and electrical hazards, blocked toilets, leaking pipes, exposed wiring, darkened stairwells where no lighting has been installed, and dirty floors. More than 500 employees of the local Olympic committee worked to fix the problems reported by the delegations.

In November 2015, Russia's track and field team was provisionally suspended from all international athletic competitions by the International Association of Athletics Federations following a World Anti-Doping Agency report into a doping program in the country. On 18 July 2016, an independent investigation commissioned by WADA reported that Russia's Ministry of Sport and Federal Security Service had operated a "state-dictated" system to implement an extensive doping program and to cover up positive samples. Based on the finding the International Olympic Committee called for an emergency meeting to consider banning Russia from the Summer Olympics. The IOC decided against completely banning Russian participation and instead decided to set additional, stricter requirements for all Russian participants entered into the Olympic Games. Originally Russia submitted a list of 389 athletes for competition. On 7 August 2016, the IOC cleared 278 athletes, while 111 were removed because of the scandal.

Printed in Great Britain
by Amazon